# I.C.U. God
# (I See You God)

James Dewees
Bridget P. Dewees, PhD

Copyright © 2018 James and Bridget Dewees

ISBN-13: 978-1727812312
ISBN-10: 172781231X

All rights reserved.

Scriptures marked KJV are taken from the KING JAMES VERSION (KJV): KING JAMES VERSION, public domain.

**Cover design and graphics**
Lonnie Brown

**Copy Layout**
Yakisha Bookard

This book is a personal testimony of the authors and does not represent the views or opinions of the hospital or staff. The authors are not medical experts and only share their personal accounts and perspectives while on the heart transplant journey.

# DEDICATION

This book is dedicated to anyone waiting on God for a special miracle. May you find strength for the journey reading this testimony.

This book is also dedicated to the special person who gave the selfless gift of organ donation—because of you, I live on to give God glory. May God bless his family and may this story encourage others to understand the need for organ donations.

# CONTENTS

ACKNOWLEDGMENTS ........................................................................ vii

## SECTION I: THE JOURNEY

FOREWORD ............................................................................. 10
INTRODUCTION ....................................................................... 13
ATTITUDE ADJUSTMENT ............................................................ 21
UNDERSTANDING GOD'S TIMING ................................................. 28
SHIFT THE ATMOSPHERE ........................................................... 34
DON'T WORRY, HAVE FAITH ....................................................... 39
ACCEPT GOD'S WILL ................................................................. 43
DON'T DOUBT, GIVE THANKS ..................................................... 47
BE GRATEFUL GOD IS WITH YOU ................................................ 52
REACH FOR THE GOAL ALWAYS! ................................................ 59
PASS THE FINAL EXAM ............................................................. 65
EDUCATE ALONG THE WAY ....................................................... 71
RECOVER BUT NEVER QUIT ....................................................... 79

## SECTION II: SPECIAL REFLECTIONS

REFLECTIONS AS A WIFE AND MOM ............................................ 86
JUSTIN WAS GOING THROUGH THIS, TOO .................................... 94

## SECTION III: THE PROMISES OF GOD

GOD'S WORD FOR THE JOURNEY .............................................. 102

## SECTION IV: SOCIAL MEDIA'S ROLE

TESTIMONIALS AND ENCOURAGEMENT FROM OTHERS ..... 109

ABOUT THE AUTHORS ............................................................. 119

# ACKNOWLEDGMENTS

Our Lord and Savior Jesus Christ

The Medical University of South Carolina— Advanced Heart Failure Team

CV-ICU Nurses

Dr. Vanbakel — Cardiologist

Dr. Katz — Transplant surgeon

Ms. Carrie — The staff cleaning team

Carol Riddell and Faye Parker — 4th Floor Concierge staff

All Prayer Warriors, Friends and Financial Supporters

Pinckney Family

Dewees Family

First Fruits Community Church

Denise Murray

Facebook Friends

Joni Grissom

# FOREWORD

*by Bridget Dewees, PhD*

In 2011, I published a book, *A 21st Century Lazarus Experience*, the book summary read:

> *"In a world filled with so many sad stories, God has given us a miracle that will lift your spirit and ignite your faith in God. A 21st Century Lazarus Experience is a testimony about ordinary people chosen for an extraordinary miracle. James and Bridget Dewees have been married for more than twenty-one years. Just like any other marriage, they have had plenty of growing pains and challenges; however, one thing always remained constant and that is their faith and love for Jesus Christ. This book is not only a testimony of the miracle God did through James, but lessons learned from a wife's point*

> *of view. It also presents a positive way to use social media for encouragement and to spread the gospel of Jesus Christ. It is my prayer that all who read will strengthen their relationship with Jesus Christ and ignite their passion to believe in miracles again."*

It is amazing how seven years later, the book summary is a continuation of the miracle and expression of James's (Jay) and my faith and love for Jesus Christ. Now, with 28 years of marriage under our belt, this story shares highlights of the transformation James and everyone connected to him experienced on the 65-day journey in the Intensive Care Unit (ICU) to a heart transplant. Included are short journals that put you in the ICU setting with James. Also included are my lessons learned, encouragement posts from friends and the scriptures that took us through the journey to transplant. James reveals his personal thoughts and how he saw God in His infinite wisdom during the stay in ICU.

James was faced with the biggest trial of his life, but when he put himself aside, he saw a big God standing behind him saying, "This isn't about you." The big God and His blueprint for our lives was revealed during this trial in ICU. We were being used to give Him all the glory and lift others along the way. When we see the hand of God in our challenges, we experience a peace that surpasses understanding. It is our prayer, that all will find this God-given peace to get through the challenges life brings and understand that with a little bit of faith and positive thinking, you can get through anything.

# INTRODUCTION

December 2, 2011, James had a near death experience indicating the seriousness of his congestive heart failure. He is a minister of music and was singing at a dear friend's wedding rehearsal. He had an arrhythmia and went into sudden cardiac death—no pulse, no heartbeat for a total of over 40 minutes. As God would have it, nurses and cardiopulmonary resuscitation (CPR) certified people were a part of the wedding party. They immediately went to work on him until the Emergency Medical Services (EMS) arrived. James was carried out of the church on a gurney as dead. After arriving at the hospital, they were able to get him stabilized. He was intubated all weekend. The doctor said only 5-10% come out of that alright and there could be brain damage. Bridget stood on faith that James would be in the 5-10%. When they extubated him on Sunday morning, he woke up as if nothing happened—limbs and memory intact.

James went back to work and lived a good life with a few minor hiccups from 2012 until 2017. In February of 2017, James's congestive heart failure took a turn for the worse. He was sick the majority of 2017, spending about 40 days in the hospital off and on, but was able to sustain and feel pretty decent on oral meds. He was encouraged to start the evaluation for a heart transplant in June 2017 and was placed on the transplant list as a low level 2 by January 2018.

On April 18, 2018, James went in for a routine checkup which included a heart cath. The results indicated that his internal pressures were very high and it was time to move forward with aggressively treating his heart failure. The doctors explained that he could not leave the hospital without some type of intervention. The choices were very slim. After 6 days of trying to bring the pressures down and to relieve the fluid off of him, he was sent to ICU with a swan catheter in his heart to constantly monitor the pressures and guide the treatment as he waited on the next steps. The severity of his heart failure moved James to 1A status and to the top of the heart transplant list.

James and Bridget lost their voice for 10 days. No one knew James was in the hospital except for immediate family and a few close friends. This was their "negotiation with God" period. The Deweeses had no choice but to trust God. On the 10th day, April 28th, they accepted the path and chose to trust God regardless of the outcome. Knowing what had to happen in order for James to receive a heart, Bridget grappled with what to pray for. One of the nurses explained that God in his infinite wisdom strategically placed James in ICU at the top of the list, because He knew another was leaving who would be selfless enough to bless him.

Once they accepted God's will for their lives, they were able to pray specifically for what they needed. Bridget posted a video on Facebook informing those connected to them about the journey they were about to embark on. She asked them to pray specifically for three things: Jay's peace, that the right heart would reach him soon, and for a successful procedure and recovery. Praying specifically is one of the key lessons Bridget learned on this journey. Bridget and James agreed to make the shift to totally trust God as soon as James said, "Bridget, they can find me the perfect heart, but if God says it is time for me to come home, I have to go—I am truly in God's hands."

James and Bridget worked daily to change the atmosphere and guarded their hearts both physically and spiritually. The family was engaged and committed to seeing James through this very challenging time. Bridget would go into the office to work several days and work from the hospital the other days; but every weekend, from April 28th until James received his heart, she and their son, Justin, packed up and spent the weekend in Charleston, SC to be with James. The family created a sense of home for James, which included Friday night family crash dates (movies and Uno). Bridget and James spent many days together just sitting still listening to music and meditating on the goodness of God. They found ways to appreciate and be thankful instead of complaining because, believe it or not, things could have been so much worse for James. Immediate family, friends, church members and co-workers supported with their time and resources.

Bridget is an avid Facebook user, but James decided to be

transparent and let others follow him on this journey of transformation. God used him to bless so many. He shared journals and tips throughout the entire stay in ICU. This was the first transformation for James, transparency – realizing that we overcome by words of our testimony. On Day 11, James wrote his first journal:

### *Journal Entry #1*
### *Day 11: April 29th*

### *Called For This Purpose*

*"Today, I realized how special I am. As I began to reminisce with some of my brothers in the ministry on today, I realized even more that I was called for this purpose. This purpose is very specific. We can recall in the scriptures how many men of God had specific purposes focused on God's plan and the up-building of His Kingdom. Abraham, Moses, David, Joshua, Elijah, and Elisha were just a few that were called to be used by God, and God worked many miracles and wonders through them. In the end, all Glory and honor was also given to God. We are living in a time where people are losing hope. Their faith in God has become so shaken with immorality and fleshly desires until they've become blinded. Blinded of the purpose that they were originally created for. God is real and he's looking for those that believe and trust in him, in spite of*

*what this world has to offer.*

*I truly believe and trust in God. My faith is strong in spite of my life's experiences. I am and have always been a living vessel ready to be used by God. I'm fortunate to have seen the manifestation and move of God throughout all my youth even up into my adulthood. As a matter of fact, I've experienced my own near death miracle in 2011. God was so graceful and merciful to bring me back with all my abilities.*

*Right now, I'm getting ready to experience something that is beyond my understanding and comprehension...a heart transplant. However...with my purpose being clear of giving glory to God, I must continue to trust and believe that even through this...everything will all work out for my good! Because of this, I can visualize that when I get through this, how blessed the Kingdom of God will be! The Bible says in Revelation 12:11 that "they overcame by the blood of the lamb, and by their testimony." This indeed is a testimony worth living for and giving. As a living vessel willing to be used by God...I will tell it wherever and whenever I get the opportunity. Thank you God for doing it one more time! To God Be Glory and Dominion forevermore! Amen!"*

ICU God is James and Bridget's continued testimony of faith, trust, and dedication to Jesus Christ. God revealed His plans or blueprint for the Deweeses in the Cardiovascular

Intensive Care Unit at the Medical University of South Carolina (MUSC), April 18, 2018 through June 25, 2018. They had the unusual opportunity to see God in a very new light. Many scriptures came alive and was revealed in a very real way. Not many people get the opportunity to spend all day and night with God for months. It was a life changing experience. James and Bridget are so humbled to be used by God in this manner. James never considered himself to be a writer, but God would give him inspirational thoughts to share while on this transformational journey. Each journal represents a specific frame of mind James was experiencing while waiting on the right heart to reach him. Meanwhile, Bridget was experiencing her own transformation about what real ministry is. She shares her insights on how lifting and supporting her husband and others kept her lifted for 65 days. ICU God was written to share insights on faith, trust and positive thinking with believers who may have lost faith along the way and with a world who may have forgotten that miracles still happen!

Nothing takes God by surprise! The Deweeses were taught that the number 8 represents new beginnings in the Bible. Everything that had a new beginning had the number 8 associated with it. All of this happened in year 2018. James received his new heart in year **8** of his congestive heart failure journey. He was in room **8** in the ICU and he took his first walk with his new heart on our 28$^{th}$ wedding anniversary. I see you God!

# ATTITUDE ADJUSTMENT

*The Bible says in everything give thanks, but it didn't say everything would feel good— Praise Him for keeping you through the challenges. Victory is coming!*

Jay

## *Inspiration from James*

The ICU is a very challenging place. Imagine embarking on a journey without a definite end date or definite outcome. All you have is your faith and your attitude. In the first several days, I was bombarded with what I felt was the scariest news I had ever received and had to deal with in my life. I had to make some serious decisions. The cardiologist was elated that I had options, but to me it was a death threat. "Mr. Dewees, you need to consider receiving a left ventricle assist device (L-VAD), which can be a bridge to heart transplant or a final destination device. You could see how long you could wait for the right heart?, but there is a possibility that your organs could be affected. Mr. Dewees, how long do you think you could wait for a heart?" WHAT?! In my entire 51 years of living, I never knew of anyone who received a heart transplant. I was very emotional. However, once I made my mind up that I was going to trust God all the way, He began to show me the "why" and gave me unbelievable strength to go through. The first thing I had to do to be successful in ICU was to check my attitude. I found that being nice goes a long way. Nurses and doctors will go beyond their job description for those who partner in their own healing. Being kind to everyone made my stay much easier and I always got what I needed in a timely manner in doing so.

God kept me in a peaceful and pleasant spirit. Friends and family would say, "God is in this room." I had several visitors also say, "James there is something special going on in here." How could that be? I was in ICU waiting on a heart transplant. This attitude comes when you let God take over your mind, body and spirit.

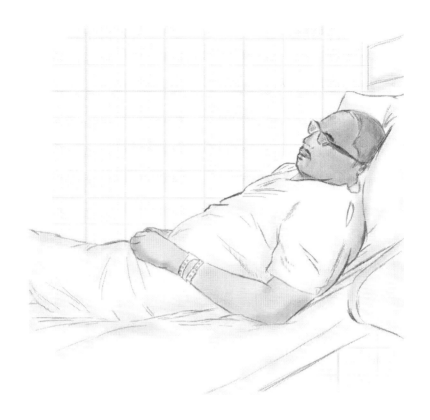

## Journal Entry #2
## Day 17: May 4<sup>th</sup>

### *He Is A Keeper*

*I'm reminded of that old spiritual that says... It's Another Day That The Lord Has Kept Me! There may be some that are asking the question... "How are you able to be so peaceful in this situation? You're waiting for something important and you're not sure when you're going to get it." Well...for those that have no hope and your faith is low, it's easy to fall into a state of being overwhelmed. However, for those of you that know of whom your hope lies (Jesus Christ), you find a sense of peace and calmness through your challenges.*

*I wanted to take a little time today to let you know that in God there is no failure! He said in His word that He will keep you in perfect peace as long as your mind is stayed on him (Isaiah 26:3). It doesn't matter what the situation is.*

*My brother and sister...there may be issues in your life that have you overwhelmed, and you aren't sure how or when you're going to get through. Here's where you have to put your trust totally in our Lord Jesus Christ. He said he will never leave you, and it's encouraging to know that He won't forsake you either (Hebrews 13:5).*

*So, lift your head up and be encouraged. God's got you and He has everything under control! Why? Because He is God, and Yes...He is a Keeper! Be Blessed!*

## Bridget's Reflection

*Bridget, we are walking in ministry. Watch how you handle everyone in this hospital.*

*Jay*

### Bridget Pinckney Dewees

Calling all preachers, missionaries and believers, the ministry is in the waiting room! I had church this morning and prayed with families! Folks are scared, worried, hurting, and lonely—I've been there! They are looking for a spark of faith and hope! Lord, I'm available!"

### Bridget Pinckney Dewees

I walked in the waiting room today to see our book on display as a choice of comfort for families. Amazing God!
Philippians 1:6 KJV: Being confident of this very thing, that he which hath begun a good work in you will perform it until the day of Jesus Christ:

---

Quickly into this journey, we realized that eyes were on us. We were representing God; our faith and trust in Him was on trial. People were watching our every move in the hospital and on social media. Social media friends said they got up the next day waiting on a post from me or Jay. Jay reminded me often that this is ministry. We have to be careful that we carry out God's will. This is His story and we are just the actors.

While Jay had his transformation in the ICU, my awakening and transformation on this journey occurred in the physical hospital waiting room on the 4th floor. God sent me two angels (Carol and Faye) in the form of concierge attendants to guide me on hospital protocol, but little did they know they were guiding me into my destiny. My eyes were opened to the needs and opportunities to serve in this small waiting room of families. In the waiting room is where I connected with several families who became my face of encouragement. Every time they saw me, they asked about the journey. We cried together, we prayed together, and we even shared each other's snacks.

In the waiting room, I realized that my 2012 publication, *A 21st Century Lazarus Experience,* brought so much comfort to hurting families. I ordered 50 copies to give away. I laid them on the tables in the chapel and on the tables in the waiting room. I met a woman named Joni who was there with a loved one every day for a couple of weeks. I gave her a copy of my first book and we just connected from there. Joni came in one day and said, "God gave me the name of your second book"—I said, really? She said, "it is a gift to you and James, your next book should be titled 'ICU God' ". Joni saw the transformation and what this journey was doing for James and me. She was a vessel used by God—yes, this book was birthed in the waiting room. I will never forget Billy, Joni, Jackie, Brenda and several others. We shared a bond and that bond was hoping and praying for a loved one to pull through.

I realized that my entire life was designed to help someone else! This is such a humbling experience. *A 21st Century Lazarus Experience* can be found all over that hospital. I gave each doctor and several nurses copies as well. I wrote that book in 2012, but God knew I needed our documented testimony to get through this journey. The impact it had on this journey was even greater than when the book was first released. It served as a reminder of what God can do. He gave us one miracle and this is just the completion of the story. It served as a tool to lift others who needed to know that miracles exist and that God hears us. Use what you've already been through to fuel your faith for the next trial! You overcome by your testimony.

# UNDERSTANDING GOD'S TIMING

## *Inspiration from James*

I don't know why God had me wait 65 days on my blessing, but looking back I see that it was all for my good. I was strengthened and renewed during my time waiting. I was able to shine God's love while waiting. This was all a part of His plan. I appreciated the gift even more because of the wait. Usually we aren't patient when it comes down to things we feel we need done right away. When we do this, we can hinder the true blessing that God has planned for us. I backed off and said, "God in your own time, my change would come." I was patient and I received my true blessing from God!

# *Journal Entry #3*
# *Day 21: May 8th*

## *Your Change is Coming*

*The Lord dropped the words of the late James Cleveland's song in my spirit on yesterday...*

*If I can hold out,*
*If I just keep the faith,*
*In God's own time...My change will come.*

*This song has encouraged me in my youth, and the words still resonate in my heart even on today. In life, we come up against obstacles that were not planned; and sometimes, these obstacles, to be real, just don't feel good. I'm sure you can agree that as Christians we don't like it when things feel bad. We want instant deliverance right away! Now, I'm a witness that there have been challenging situations and trials where God stepped in and I did get instant deliverance. Praise God!*

*However, there have been struggles that I've faced where I had to patiently wait on God's timing. It didn't feel good, but I trusted in God! It didn't change overnight, but I still trusted in God! I didn't fully understand what was going on, but I was reminded of Proverbs 3:15 that says, "Trust in the Lord with all your heart and lean not to your own understanding." Eventually, God brought me through and I had the affirmation that nobody could've brought me through but God!! Hallelujah! On this Christian journey, it is definite that we are going to have test and trials, but it's through these test and trials that God makes us stronger.*

*Psalms 27:14 expresses that if we wait on the Lord, and be of good courage, he shall and will strengthen our hearts. In conclusion...in the words of James Cleveland, "Hold out (wait) just a little while longer! These heavy burdens (trials, sickness, whatever it may be...) they will soon pass over!" So just run the race my Brother and keep the faith my Sister. Why? Because in God's own time...your change will surely come! May God continue to Bless and Keep you!*

## *Bridget's Reflection*

James was in ICU 65 days. I saw all of those hospital rooms turn over at least 6 times during our stay there. This journey will make you see life so differently. While you are waiting on God, there will be times when others get their blessing long before you do. You could be waiting on healing, marriage, jobs, or children, but you learn to honestly celebrate others and pray for their needs even when yours hasn't come yet.

Only through God can you deny your wants and pray for others. I've been there so many times in my life—I've helped and ushered others into blessings that I myself was waiting on. I can honestly say, I've never had an ill jealous bone in my body. Even when others would purposely be a Peninnah—say things to taunt and provoke me during the waiting period, I still prayed (I Samuel 1:2). Every battle prepares you for the war! Because of those experiences, I was fully armed to win this war. Wait on the Lord and be of good courage—your victory could very well be in the way you wait on God! Don't worry about those getting blessed ahead of you, don't worry about those talking negative, or the doubters. You must still believe that everything that happens is for your good and God's glory. Remember, even as blessed as Peninnah was, inwardly she was jealous of the hurting Hannah.

God is strategic and His timing is impeccable! Looking back over this year, I now see how He put everything in place for us to be able to handle this trial! I am a living witness that God won't ever give you more than you can handle! I feel special knowing that I'm His child and everything works for my good, even if it doesn't feel good! From day one, God let me know this was all His plan!

I had a dream early April and saw Jay sitting with a look of disbelief as his cardiologist told him some news. I woke up and told Jay the dream and to please take it easy, don't do anything to put yourself in the hospital. Two weeks later he went in for a routine heart cath and they kept him! When they told us, "It's time. You will need a heart transplant sooner than later"—that look on Jay's face was the one I saw in the dream. Right then, I knew God had us and this was the path.

As I mentioned earlier, for the first ten days, we couldn't talk about it! I lost my voice, but God reminded me of my role in this story—to tell it and give Him glory! So, I posted my first video about what was going on and for 70 days, I've been doing just that! But not only on social media. I've given out over 50 books and shared our story with several hurting families in the waiting rooms. God immediately showed us the purpose for this journey!

It was never about Bridget, Jay and Justin. We were chosen to do a work. I look at how God allowed me to finish the semester and make it to summer semester, when the campus was least busy. Justin made it successfully through 9th grade and Jay's driving restrictions ended the month Justin went back to school! 2018 summer vacation was like no other. We got a heart transplant!

God is amazing and if we just trust the plans He has for us, it will work out in His timing! And the timing of placing Jay at the top of the list to receive a healthy heart was just amazing!

I've quoted Jeremiah 29:11 over and over, but my God has shown it to me!

*For I know the thoughts that I think toward you, saith the Lord, thoughts of peace, and not of evil, to give you an expected end. (Jeremiah 29:11 KJV)*

## SHIFT THE ATMOSPHERE

### *Inspiration from James*

I had to shift my thoughts, so the only way to do this was to make my atmosphere a positive atmosphere. My wife and I touched and agreed that we were doing ministry in this hospital and we had to be so careful of how we managed our atmosphere. Going through the heart transplant process was not an easy process to face; so, to begin, I had to guard my heart from anything that would form doubt. Although I am a very positive person, I didn't let too many people in during this critical time. I needed my atmosphere to be just right for God to do the work. The power of positive thinking and a little bit of faith can move mountains!

## *Journal Entry #4*
## *Day 28: May 15th*

### *Mind Over Matter*

*Well, tomorrow will be approximately 1 month since I've been in the hospital. Under normal circumstances, if I focused on the negatives of my situation, I would be livid, but I can truly say that God is keeping me! I believe it's true that your mind and how you think plays an important part with how you deal and go through life's situations in general. If you're not careful, you can find yourself sinking into the ground filled with quicksand concerning anything that comes up in life. However, in most cases, when you look back, you realize that it really wasn't that serious and it wasn't even worth the frustration.*

*I chose, through this process, to stay positive. I believe that there is purpose for everything that we experience in life. These experiences are put in place to strengthen the believer's faith so that when other challenges come up, we won't be so alarmed. This is what gives me peace...knowing that I'm in God's hands and that He is in control, no matter what happens in my life.*

*This leads me to my last thought. What has really been helpful to me through this process is keeping my mind and thoughts on spiritual things. As I expressed in one of my earlier posts...God will keep you in perfect peace as long as your mind is focused on Him (Isaiah 26:3). With this in mind, please note that this doesn't mean that I'm taking this heart transplant lightly. This procedure is very serious. Nevertheless, throughout all of my life's experiences, God has shown himself to be right there by my side to bring me through. He hasn't changed and He's never failed me. Keeping my mind on these thoughts allow me to stay in a realm of peace that surpasses even my own understanding!*

*I pray that this post encourages you to focus on those things that are positive in your life. I'm a witness that if you do, you'll feel so much better!*

*Please take the time to reflect on this scripture:*

*"Finally my brethren, whatsoever things are true, whatsoever things are honest, whatsoever things are pure, whatsoever things are lovely, whatsoever things are of good report, if there be any virtue, and if there be any praise, think on these things" (Philippians 4:8).*

*Once again thank you all for your prayers! Be encouraged and know that God is still on the throne and He is in control! Be Blessed!*

## *Bridget's Reflection*

Your expectations drive your attitude; your attitude drives your peace. It is so important to set clear expectations when dealing with a hard trial. Life all around you must go on. People need to work, kids go to school, and the church must roll on! It's easy to expect life everywhere to pause when you're going through, but it is important to meet everyone where they are. Keep your peace at all times. Always look to God for your needs—He taps the most unexpected people to come to your rescue. He will use a stranger on an elevator to lift you, the cleaning lady to pray with you, and a stranger to provide funds. God wants us to totally depend and trust in Him. So many of us are putting total trust in jobs, pastors, friends and even family. Yes, we need our village and I am so grateful for my network, but my expectations are in God. God is the only one who is even capable to never leave or forsake you!

One of the most valuable skills God gave me through this storm was how to go to my place of peace. Finding this place of peace starts with believing that everything that happens to you is ultimately for your good when you are following God. The struggle is hard until you accept God's will for your life. Even Jesus struggled with his death on the cross, but when he fully gave over to the will of the Father, he gained real peace. This same peace Jesus had on the cross is available to all believers!

God has everything we need to carry out His will! I

adopted a new philosophy that helped me get through: If it bothers my peace, I'm not dealing with it! When in a fight for your life, you can't associate/entertain doubters, haters, and peace-breakers. Show them who God is by how you handle daily situations. My husband practiced this the entire time he was in ICU. I remember one day our son came in ICU in a horrible teenage mood. Dad said, "I love you Justin, but please step outside and get yourself together—you are disturbing my peace." Yes, sometimes you have to put those closest to you out for a while. Justin got it together quick!

# DON'T WORRY, HAVE FAITH

## *Inspiration from James*

When I found out that I had to stay in ICU, I saw this as a very bad problem. It was going to hinder my agenda and things I felt I had to do, things I felt I wanted to do, and things I felt that I couldn't do. I had to take my mind off of what was wrong and start to think only on the goal, which was to get better so that I could enjoy the fullness of my life.

I had to work on focusing daily. I had to say to myself that God is with me and I am going to come out successful. I truly believed that everything that happened to me was for my good and working for my good. This is the promise of the believer: God is with you ALWAYS!

## *Journal Entry #5*
## *Day 32: May 19th*

### God Is With You

*When I think of hiking, I can imagine the ups and downs of the trail. I imagine hills and sometimes valleys you may come across, depending on the location of the trail. I see the trees and the greenery that may sometime hide the actual trails you are following. I imagine the wild life that comes out to welcome you into their habitat. Most of all…I can imagine the opportunity of stepping away from the everyday normal life in hopes of clearing your mind from it all.*

*This same picture is how I visualize Life. We are all on a trail, and on this trail comes life's ups and downs, hills and valleys. As we travel along this trail, sometimes we enter the pasture of some pretty big trees, situations and trials that may cause you to lose focus on your purpose and direction in which you are traveling. In most cases we are often trying to find ways where we can step away from it all just to feel a sense of inner peace.*

*The bottom line…life alone is not easy. It's not a fairy tale. It doesn't always feel the way we think it should feel; but, when you find that special relationship with God, He somehow knows how to make life feel so much better. Sometimes, the trail or goal may seem a little longer, and sometimes hectic, before you really get to know God's purpose for you.*

*However...once you get it, you're able to deal with life's pressures with an epiphany that says hey...I can do this! It's then you realize how blessed you truly are.*

*A word of reassurance for you not to give up on your journey. Stay focused. Be diligent and keep on pressing forward. Most of all...be encouraged! God is right there and He is willing to carry you through whatever trial or struggle you may be facing in your life. Just know that it's through this journey that you begin to understand the plan that God has for you. One of my favorite scriptures states, "And we know that all things work together for good to them that love God, to them who are the called according to his purpose" (Romans 8:28). I stand on God's Word! And you should too!*

## *Bridget's Reflection*

Every day was a brand new opportunity for God to answer our prayers and we didn't even talk about yesterday. I received so many compliments in reference to management of this challenge. However, let me be totally transparent—I wake up grateful for a new day, but I am not always pumped and on a spiritual high every day. Just like all of us, I had to make a conscious choice to be encouraged, to be happy, to be grateful, and to believe. I had to repeat God's Word concerning me, even with tears in my eyes. One thing I've learned on this transplant journey for sure—life is all about choices, starting with your daily attitude. So, start your day by choosing to be more than a conqueror, victorious and encouraged! Make sure you have seeds planted that can sprout up when you need them.

Through my transparency, I realized that so many are dealing with very hard things in their own lives, but don't have a trusted friend or family member to share it with. Please get closer to your family and friends and start trusting again. You will feel so much better living with nothing to hide. Yes, folks are sometimes evil, but if you pray, God will show you who's real and who's in it for the ride—either way you're coming out victorious!

# ACCEPT GOD'S WILL

## *Inspiration from James*

I had to convince myself that I was in the will of God, even though I couldn't understand at the beginning the purpose of what was going on. As I reconditioned my thinking, I realized that it was best for me to trust Him and that it was all going to work out for my good! This is where I had to put all of my faith to work. "Faith is the substance of things hoped for, the evidence of things not seen" (Hebrews 11:1). Can you trust Him, when you can't see Him? God has your best interest in His heart, and everything is for your good.

## Journal Entry #6
## Day 39: May 26th

### No More Than I Can Bear

So many have heard about my near death experience in 2011. Yes...God allowed me to walk away from Death still whole and in my right mind! However...many haven't heard what brought me to this near death experience. I would like to share just a little of it with you on today.

During the week prior to my near death experience, my family was called into the hospital to discuss next steps to be done with my mother, who was there for serious health reasons. Also, I had some major issues going at work, as well as with life in general, that I took to heart. The burdens began to feel overwhelmingly hard to bear. As a result, I started forgetting important things, like my bank password and password to my company computer. These were signs of what was to come, but I ignored them.

(Fast forward to after the near death experience.)

It's hard to explain, but when I woke up on Sunday morning, the burdens that I felt prior to the near death experience were gone! It was as if God took the pain and heartache that I had felt and lifted it. Everything that I was forgetting, I remembered afterwards. I even had the strength to endure the passing of my mother, which happened not too far afterwards.

*God gave me the assurance that He was with me through this trying time (Hebrews 13:5).*

*In my younger days, I often heard the saying that God wouldn't put on you no more than you can bear. Today, I can truly say that through my challenge in 2011, with God's love, compassion and grace, my burdens were lifted. It was through that experience that I feel comforted in knowing that God is still with me. Even now, He knows how much I can bear. Thank You God for your loving kindness and your tender mercies! Great Is Your Faithfulness!*

## *Bridget's Reflection*

God sends the perfect storms already pre-planned according to His will and designed for our growth. He has a perfect will for us. I realized that every single day is a gift and I had to be careful how I unwrapped it. Last year (2017), my mom, Hazel Pinckney, spent some time with us during Jay's sickness. She shared the Bible story of Hezekiah and reminded me to live a life that will make God change His mind about my situation. Hezekiah was sick unto death and was told to get things in order because he was going to die and not live. Hezekiah turned his face to the wall and prayed, but he did something else. He reminded God of how he walked before

Him in truth and how he had done well in His sight. Hezekiah worshiped God with his life and God honored that! While he was praying, God heard him and changed His mind giving him fifteen more years (2 King 20:1-6).

I don't know how long any of us have to live, but I do know that God has changed His mind about our situation a few times. By all medical standards, Jay should be gone, but I truly believe he lives a life that is pleasing in the sight of God. We are not made to be perfect and we can't live good enough to deserve His goodness, but I plan to spend the rest of my life trying. I want to live a life that makes God change his mind about my situation.

# DON'T DOUBT, GIVE THANKS

## *Inspiration from James*

My greatest strength came from me knowing that God was with me in the midst of the valley. Although I was in the critical care unit, I was still very mobile. I could walk, eat, and clean up all by myself. The only thing very sick on me was my heart, which is a miracle in itself. God kept my organs strong enough to endure the 24-hour IV drips and the medicine load that kept my heart strong. I always saw the silver lining. I constantly reminded myself that I could be so much worse. I got to the place where I had the freedom to walk around ICU all by myself. I began to give thanks for where I was before I had even gotten the heart.

My congestive heart failure started in 2010 with an enlarged heart and in 2011 I had a near death experience. This journey fueled my faith in 2018. I would often look back over where God brought me from and the one thing that got me through was praise. My wife and I laughed when we saw a work of art right outside my ICU room named the "Praise House". Room 8 became the praise house! Strength comes when you can praise God at all times!

### *Journal Entry #7*
### *Day 42: May 29th*

### *I Will Not Stop Giving God The Praise*

*I believe there's power in praising God! It doesn't matter what it looks like...I believe if you praise God, you get results. Today, my father visited me, and throughout our conversation, we were thanking God for giving me strength and keeping me covered while being here in ICU. As an example...I have been fortunate to take walks about 3 times throughout the day just to keep my physical strength up while waiting for the big procedure. This is truly a blessing, considering my reason for being here in the first place.*

*As I have expressed in times past, when you praise God for what He's doing at all times, meaning through the good and the not so good, you will keep seeing the blessings of God manifesting in your life. The scripture says, "God inhabits the praises of his children" (Psalms 22:3-5). I encourage you to keep on sending your praises up to God. You'll find that your blessings aren't too far behind! Once again...thank you all for your prayers! They are working.*

## *Reflection from Bridget*

Fear and doubt will keep you living beneath your God-given privileges! When you are on a faith walk, never get distracted by the ones who won't and can't walk with you. God is only creating an atmosphere where He can work. And don't be surprised if it's just you and Him many times! Your environment is so critical to maintaining a level of faith during a challenge. Jay and I have been very careful of what we entertain and what we allow in our environment.

You have the power to create an environment conducive for faith to work. Jay told me, "If anyone is willing to dump negativity on me right now, they don't care about me." I've seen him stop a conversation right in its track. You control your atmosphere. One ill thought planted could take days or weeks to uproot! Funny how you start to immediately identify negativity—it feels like a pin sticking you. It's intentional work to stay positive in a negative world! Remember, your wealthy place of growth was designed for you only. If God puts you there, it's where you belong for now. Stay in peace.

God really gave me a lesson in trust this time! I was in a place where all I could do was make plans for the current day. I felt like the disciples when Jesus told them in Matthew 6:34, *"Take therefore no thought for the morrow: for the morrow shall take thought for the things of itself."* It really isn't a bad place to be when you learn to let go and let God!

Finally, don't be afraid of "No" when you are going for that ultimate "Yes"! *"Faith is the substance of things hoped for and the evidence of things not seen" (Hebrews 11:1).* So many times we are afraid of just putting it out there; so, we pray a blanket prayer "God's will be done!" It is His will that you *ask* specifically for what you want even if you can't see it. If God's answer is "No," that's His perfect will at the time. Your steps are ordered! Although we love open doors, God speaks to us through opened and closed doors. We really have to learn to trust God.

## Bridget Pinckney Dewees

On April 18th, my husband was facing a tough thing—I put a video out there asking specifically for what we needed and many of you touched and agreed. My God did every single thing just as I asked: for Jay's peace, the right heart, a successful process and speedy recovery! Lose the fear and pray bold prayers, my friend! Don't worry about what if it doesn't happen, think about what if it happens! Bishop Bonner, one of our previous pastors, would say, "God is going to do what you say, not what your enemy says and not what the devil says. The miracle is in your mouth." Don't let fear and doubt cripple you from just saying IT! Ask God specifically for what you want and begin thanking Him for it right away.

# BE GRATEFUL GOD IS WITH YOU

## *Inspiration from James*

So many times in life we have the tendency to focus on all of the negatives that we face until we are blinded to seeing all of the true blessings that are flowing all around us. If the enemy can keep you bound with low self-esteem, or thinking that you're never going to be successful, or even thinking that you're not liked by anyone, then he feels he's won the victory over your life! While I was waiting in ICU, I was determined not to give him my victory! I knew that one way of doing this was to give God praise even in the state I was in. Yes, I was waiting on a heart, but even with that I knew I could still find more than one thing to be thankful for. I also found out that my joy came through my Praise!

> *"I will Bless the Lord at all times, and His praises shall continue to be in my mouth!"*
> *(Psalm 34:1)*

ICU is a critical care unit where the sickest of the sick are placed. Many receive their healing on the other side with their maker. I experienced the screams and cries of family members as they said good-bye to loved ones. Nothing changes you more than a bout with mortality. I realized that I wanted to live and I believed I was going to live, but death was often all around me. There were moments I had to encourage myself. There were times I would remember scriptures and stories of the Bible where you saw God at work. There were other times I would reminisce on the things God did for me personally. These testimonies helped me to overcome. They always served as an encouragement that He would do it again!

## *Journal Entry #8*
## *Day 47: June 3rd*

### *I'm So Grateful*

*I was just reminiscing on the song Be Grateful, written by Walter Hawkins, and I began to feel the presence of God rising up on the inside! While being here in ICU, I am still grateful. As I expressed not too long ago...I get the opportunity to walk around ICU, and I see so many critical situations around me. I mean...there are some very serious health issues. With this in mind, I realize that I could have been in a much worse condition than I am, even while waiting for a heart. For this cause...God...I am so grateful! I'm grateful that you are keeping me intact, both physically and mentally! I'm grateful that I still have my activities and that I still have a mind to give you praise! I'm grateful that you are keeping my family even through the midst of this test! Lord...I'M SO GRATEFUL! Is there anybody else out there that's grateful? Then, help me give God praise! Hallelujah!*

*"Yea though I walk through the valley and shadow of death, I will fear no evil"*
*(Psalm 23)*

## *Journal Entry #9*
## *Day 55: June 11th*

### *God is With Me*

*Most seasoned Christians can relate when I say that one of the first chapters out of the Bible learned was Psalms 23. It is a chapter that flows really well, so as a child it was easy to retain, even though at the time we didn't understand the depths of what it really meant. It was only as I got older that the Lord allowed me insight bit by bit. Even now, I'm still receiving revelation from God on what certain verses mean to me based on my personal experiences.*

*Just on last week I had an awareness concerning where I am and the extent of what I am around. To keep it real...ICU is no joke! There are some very, very sick people in this place. I was taking my daily stroll on last Monday evening, and noticed that there were several people coming up to the room next to my room. At first, I didn't think too much of it, though in my mind it did seem a little stranger than usual. I got back to my room, and not too long after, a good friend stopped by to see about me. About 30 minutes later, as we were talking we began to hear a woman crying pretty intensely. This then signified that the patient next door had expired. I would be remiss to say that this didn't play with my thoughts for a moment. It was totally unexpected. However, I thank God for bringing a very familiar scripture back to my remembrance and I quote, "Yea though I walk through the valley of the shadow of death, I will fear no evil: for thou (God) art with me; thy rod and thy staff they comfort me." Yes...this same scripture that I have read probably thousands of times, literally resonated within and once again gave me peace and comfort. God was reassuring me not to take my eyes off of the purpose and goal of my intentions. He has brought me this far, and His word stands assured that He will not leave me, nor forsake me.*

*In conclusion, I'm sure many of you will agree with me when I say that the Bible is so awesome! There are so many lessons to be learned from it, and it doesn't matter how many times you read it, God always allows for new revelation of His word to be seen, if you're only opened to receiving it. My brothers and sisters...always remember that God is a strong tower! It doesn't matter what we go through or experience, He is a refuge and shield in times of trouble.*

*Please join in and help me with this moment of praise; Lord...we thank you for strength! We thank you for your shelter! We are encouraged to know that it is through your power and authority that we are comforted! You Are Worthy To Be Praised! God Bless!*

## *Reflection from Bridget*

I found healing in sharing my most intimate thoughts while on this journey. I will be forever grateful for the many lessons I've learned. God taught me that my strength increased when I gave Him the glory. So, I showed my gratefulness by posting stories of love, encouragement and even frustration. Many of my friends responded in ways that lifted me. My strength came from God, but He used an entire village to carry us. People gave of their time and resources to make sure I had what I needed to support Jay and Justin.

This experience changed my perspective on worship. I will forever worship God with my life, my giving and my helping those in need. If you ever find yourself in the caregiver role, just know you play a key role in the outcome for your loved one. Don't ever take the role lightly. Find ways to be grateful and God will give you the strength to get through it.

# REACH FOR THE GOAL ALWAYS!

## *Inspiration from James*

Not knowing that I was only one week away from my blessing, I found myself getting a little weary of the journey. Many times in life, we are so close to the breakthrough and we give up. I began to wonder how much longer could I stay upbeat and positive. I had to shake myself because I knew I couldn't live in this mood too long. We are human and we will have days like these in life, but those are the days you have to rely on God's strength even more. I told myself that God was going to accomplish what He set out to do. Remember God's Word, speak it over your situation and then accept God's will and timing for your life.

## Journal Entry #10
## Day 59: June 15th

### What Do You Do When

Hello, People of God!! Well...It's been about 60 days of waiting in ICU for the heart transplant process to begin. As you all know, I've been staying pretty positive as well as being transparent on this journey. It has definitely been an experience thus far; yet I'm still giving God praise for keeping me in the midst of it all!

So...the big question of the day is what do you do when you're waiting for a breakthrough, but receiving it seems to be a little longer than expected? Well...here are 3 steps that I feel have helped me along the way through my waiting period:

1. First and foremost...falling back to the Word of God gives me strength to stand on His promises even when the outcome seems to be a little lengthy. Hebrews 11:1 states that "Faith is the substance of things hoped for, the evidence of things not seen."

2. Sometimes while waiting you have to speak over yourself and encourage yourself in the Lord. "Remember self...it's through my faith that everything will work out for my good!"

3. Last, but not least, remembering that God's timing is always the right timing. He may not come when you think He should, but when He does come, He's always on time!

*Romans 5:1 states that because we are justified by faith, we have peace with God through our Lord Jesus Christ. We've got to hold on to our faith, no matter what it looks like! God promises peace through our faith.*

*Note...it's the enemy's job to try and bring discouragement through our situation because he knows that God's promises are true. He will try to bring a sense of doubt to your mind to get you to give up on God before your blessing comes. But I want you to say with me that the devil is a liar! What God has for you...it is for YOU!*

*So recapping back to the question...what do you do when you're waiting for a breakthrough? Stand on God's Word and keep the faith. Continue to speak over yourself that it will work out in my favor because I have the favor of God over my life! And lastly...hold on to the promises of God. In God's own time your change will surely come because His promises stand assure! Keep on holding on people of God! Your blessing is right around the corner!*

## *Reflection from Bridget*

**Bridget Pinckney Dewees**

Today was just full of Love! People are just overwhelming me with their support, prayers and words of encouragement! Cards via mail, notes via inboxes, texts, calls! I know you are lifting us—we feel it! I got my hair washed and my stylist still won't take money-I stopped by the grocery store—ran into my Pastor and his wife, Abraham & Tyjuana Belanger— who paid for my food! I am humbled! It doesn't feel like day #49 at all! Thank you everyone!

When reaching for the goal, God will give you the strength you need even if it comes from a stranger. So many friends and family members supported us through this entire journey. My sister, Sheila, and brother, Ray, made trips down to help me often. My siblings raised funds to help with our day-to-day expenses and hotel stays close to the hospital. My brother-in-law, Clay, would provide haircuts for Jay while in ICU. God gave us so many prayer warriors from all over the nation.

On one of the most draining days, God used a total stranger to lift and replenish me. As Justin and I got off the elevator after eating breakfast, a woman on the elevator asked where we were from. I told her we are locals and my husband is in the hospital down the street, so we are on our way. We got off the elevator, she stopped, asked me his name and said she would pray for him. At first, I thought what a common thing to say these days. She was a beautiful blonde lady—she had a teen daughter who was just as nice. She looked in my eyes and saw the weariness and said, "I was a nurse and my daughter right here had a very long stay in the hospital, so I understand." She immediately hugged me right there in the crowd—she held me so tight until I cried. I whispered to her, "He needs a heart transplant," releasing the tiredness and gaining the strength I needed for this day. She prayed and then her teen daughter hugged me! I would have never thought of her as God's arms, but God put her on that elevator with me. Until God raptures the church, His spirit will prevail—God has us! He really won't put more on us than we can bear, and when He thinks it too heavy, He will send the arms you need! This taught me to make myself available for his use every day—I just might be the arms that lift a burden.

 I was so overwhelmed by the outpour of love from family, friends, and even strangers. Many funded all of the extra travel and hotel expenses associated with a 75 day hospital stay. It was so hard for me to receive so much from others because I have been a giver my whole life. God spoke to me and said that it was my season to receive all He had for me and to let others be a blessing. Once I got over myself, I realized that there is more love in this world than hate and to let love thrive.

## PASS THE FINAL EXAM

### *Inspiration from James*

When I think about Day 65, the day I found out about my new heart, I realized that I was taking a final exam; but this was no ordinary test. This was a test on everything I knew and believed about God. I believe each of us will have final exams or days of reconciliation with God. When those times come, all you can do is pull from everything you know about God, His word, and your previous experiences.

*Journal Entry #11*
*Day 65: June 21st*

**This Is Not A Normal Test**

*Hello All! Once again...I thank God for*

*your prayers and encouraging words. They have all worked together, along with the strength of God, to keep me focused while waiting on the heart transplant. As I reminisce on the concept of me enduring a major heart surgery, God gave me a scenario that helps me to see the positive outcome of it all. I felt lead to share it with you and I pray that it blesses you just as it has blessed me.*

*Imagine starting the beginning of a school year. Once started you begin to learn about certain subjects, whatever they may be. Not too long after that you begin having quizzes and test concerning the subjects learned. However...after all the learning, quizzes and test, at the end of the year, you have one big test you have to prepare for...the Final Exam. This Exam determines whether or not you are prepared to transition to your next level of school, or even graduate to your next phase in life. Sometimes it takes you recapping on all of your notes, previous quizzes and test to make sure you have retained what's needed to pass the test. It's all in how you study and prepare that validates the outcome of your goal, which is passing that Exam! I feel this scenario fits my personal life's situation to the "T". In my life,*

*I have had some life learning experiences. I've had some little hurdles (quizzes) and some pretty big trials (tests), which all have strengthened my faith in God, knowing that it was only through Him that I got over (Acts 17:28). Now, I feel that I am coming up against one of the biggest challenges in my life. Nevertheless, knowing that everything happens for a purpose, I feel that all my life experiences (trials and tests) have prepared me for this big Exam. As a matter of fact...I believe that God allows all that we go through in life to be a help meet so that when we're challenged with that next big test, we have enough ammunition to come through victorious! Romans 8:37 states that, "Nay, in all of these things we are more than conquerors through him that loved us." Final thought...don't take your life's up and downs, your trials, and challenges for granted. Use them as a study guide (ammunition) for that big Exam that may be coming up in your life, if it hasn't already. How you prepare throughout your life determines how successful you are in passing the big exams in your life. God Bless You!*

## *Reflection from Bridget*

For the first time in 65 days, I decided to meet my colleagues for dinner; so, my cell phone was on vibrate in my purse. I had just left the hospital after spending my normal Wednesday with Jay; so, I knew he was fine and all was well.

Meanwhile, at the hospital, Jay was getting ready to eat dinner, but it was quickly taken away and he was told to go NPO (nothing by mouth). "There is a possibility," they said, "and it's a good one." Jay was so calm and collected. The next 24 hours was exam time. He'd been prepping for 65 days and now the finale begins.

Jay said he called me three times and found it unusual that I didn't answer right away. Let me remind you…I'd been living with cell phone in hand for two months, but on the evening I decided to REST and RELAX, God said NOW! That's a lesson in trust right there! So, at dinner for some reason, I couldn't eat either—I wanted to eat, but my appetite completely left me. I decided to just visit the team of colleagues and catch up while they ate.

After about thirty minutes or so, I felt this nudge to look at my phone and realized it was in my purse and not a part of the dinner table silverware. I pulled it out to see three missed calls from Jay. I quickly dialed him back and he said, "Hey, I've been calling you. We might have a possibility." "What did you just say?" "They stopped me from eating and are preparing me for a possibility." Jay named the new heart "a maybe." He would never say, "This is it!" He was told not to get his hopes up because so many things had to go right for this to happen; so, flat-footed he remained!

After my colleagues picked me up off the table, I asked one of them to say a quick prayer for me. Dee stepped up and did just that. I wanted to jet back to the hospital, but Jay insisted I go home, pack a bag and come back later. He said, "We have time and Bridget this is still a maybe." I drove down I-26 praising God all the way home—I don't even know how I got home that evening! It was indeed me and Jesus!

I headed back to the hospital ready to spend the night in ICU with Jay! When I walked in the unit, our medical family was high fiving and celebrating like it was Christmas. I'm saying to myself, "It's a maybe. Why are they so excited?" Right then, I knew this was more than a maybe, we were about to go on the ride of our lives and God was about to answer those specific prayers everyone was sending up. It was time to get ready!

When I saw Jay, he had such a calm look of purpose and

resolve. I've never seen such strength and faith in action as I did on this journey with Jay. I saw what I always knew he was called to be! From the day I married Jay, I knew he had a special purpose in the earth. So many times he doubted his own abilities, but I never did! The nurses brought me a pillow and blanket and let me sleep in the recliner that night! We didn't sleep or talk much because our "maybe" was coming.

What a journey of self-discovery and manifestation of the power of God! After 65 days and on our 28th anniversary weekend, Jay received a new heart! Jay was taken to the operating room around 4:30 p.m. the next evening. We were told the donor heart arrived around 6:00 p.m. and by 8:00 p.m. Jay had a new heart.

Dr. Katz came out to find me in the waiting room with the biggest smile on his face. He told me everything went fantastic and James was doing well. The heart began to pump without priming or shocking as soon as they connected it to Jay's blood! Oh, the praises that went up on that 4th floor! Lives will never be the same! Nurses and hospital staff came in all day to wish Jay well! Many said they'd never had a patient quite like him! I thought to myself all night, the only limits on God are the ones we place on Him! For the rest of my life I will give God praise for this wonderful miracle.

## EDUCATE ALONG THE WAY

### *Inspiration from James*

My wife and I were always seeking knowledge on my Congestive Heart Failure (CHF) issue. Throughout this journey, we realized that so many of our friends and family did not understand the value of organ transplant. So, we shared a lot of information about the process. We didn't have a problem questioning the doctors if there was something we didn't understand. While being in ICU, I made sure I was very familiar with the procedures and the medicines I was taking. There was one point where the nurse's noticed and would say, "Mr. Dewees, we need to give you a nurse badge because you're on top of it and you know what's going on."

I believe the fact that I was familiar with the process assisted with everything staying on track. I realized that staying mobile kept me healthy and sane. Because I was so mobile, this helped me to have a speedy recovery after the transplant. For example, they pulled the breathing tube out of my mouth and I was walking on day 2! This kind of recovery from a heart transplant was rarely seen in ICU! God specifically ordained this path for me. The transplant surgeon explained to my wife that the donor heart arrives cold and on ice. They usually have to prime it, pump it and massage it for it to start working; BUT as soon as they connected the heart to my blood, it started beating immediately with no intervention.

The hospital asked me if I would agree to participate in an educational documentary to benefit new students; so they interviewed me prior to and after the transplant. I was able to speak directly with the doctor who did the filming of my transplant and oh the excitement on his face when he explained how unusual this was. He said that they were prepared to shock the heart, but it just took off beating once it was connected to my blood. This gave me an assurance that God was in total control. I left my wife and family that night with such peace knowing that I would be okay on the other side of transplant.

Passing this kind of exam only comes from knowing what God can do, either from previous testimonies or from your faith in the Word of God. I can't guarantee you that every outcome will be the same as mine, but I can guarantee that God is able and He loves you! I went into this challenge believing that I was in God's hands and His perfect will. I was going to be just fine either way God decided to go with me. We have to trust the plans God has for us. I am so humbled that God used me in this way to give Him all of the glory!

In conclusion, I praise God for giving me wisdom to get through this very challenging trial. I saw the hands of God at work while in ICU and today I am a much stronger and better person than I was before going into ICU. I pray that my lessons learned and coping strategies will help assist you with any challenge in your life!

### *Journal Entry #12*
### *Day 69: June 25th*

### Well… He Did It Again!

*Hello to all my brothers and sisters! I stand here today to say that our God is such an Awesome God! He did everything He promised he would do, and I mean Everything! I am so humbled. I kept the faith all the way to the operating table, but when I came out I was still blown away! No complications, no setbacks. Everything ran smoothly! I was sitting up the next day in a chair, and the following day I was walking around ICU again! Hallelujah! When the praises of God go up…His blessings has got to come down!!*

*I give a special shout to my lovely wife Bridget! She was supportive throughout this whole transaction! I cannot and will not forget my beautiful diamond! A gift given to me from God! And as she expressed it…what an awesome gift of receiving the heart transplant on our 28th wedding anniversary weekend! We will cherish this moment for the rest of our lives! The Power of Positive Thinking Mixed With A Little Bit Of Faith Can Move*

*Mountains! Thanking you all for your prayers and praises! The prayers of the righteous avails much! What a mighty God we serve! Be Blessed!*

---

## *Reflection from Bridget*

When many of our friends and even family heard that Jay was waiting on a heart transplant, they went into absolute panic mode. Several thought he was on breathing tubes, could barely walk or possibly taking his last few breaths. Their faith was shattered in many cases. So, when we would post upbeat things, or even the fact that I could continue working through the wait shocked many. God reminded me that teaching is my gift and the core of who I am. I was to use this experience to help others understand the journey, both from a natural as well as spiritual perspective. I started a series of informative Facebook posts called "Transplant Education." My first post was written to primarily calm the masses—hey, we are OK, Jay is doing the right thing at the right time.

---

**Bridget Pinckney Dewees**

Transplant Education: Several have asked me questions that lead me to believe that many don't understand the organ transplant process. We are here to not only be examples spiritually, but to educate anyone we can along the way. In order to get a transplant, one must go through an extensive physical to include organ checks, blood checks, checks for possible diseases and more to make sure your body can handle this extensive invasion. Jay went through the evaluation process fall 2017 while in the hospital and a few more checks in 2018 when the doctors realized his situation had declined. There is a period in heart failure when you have to make a decision on timing. You can't be too well, you won't want it and you can't be too sick, the medical team won't grant it. Jay has reached that middle place where his heart is very sick and is being treated with meds intravenously, but his other organs are strong enough for transplant. Even here, the hands of God are on him, keeping him strong both in mind and body. There are three levels on the transplant list (2, 1B, 1A), Jay moved from 2 to 1b to now 1A in about 6 months. Jay is so resilient— we knew this was a possibility, but was still shocked when it happened. I advise anyone dealing with a medical diagnosis to do your own research, ask plenty of questions and be your number one advocate. Jay even kept track of meds given to him while in the hospital and has caught slight mistakes himself. So, we feel very blessed to have an option that will give Jay a quality life for many years if God says so!

---

As the days went by and I began to learn more about the process, I was just amazed! We believed God for complete healing, but we never thought this would be the path for us. I was encouraged once again to TRUST God. He knew the plans He had for us since the beginning. We were chosen to give Him glory because He knew we would. As we progressed through the waiting period, I noticed that several people would offer condolences or a form of pity. I knew they didn't mean any harm, but I felt the need to let everyone know that being able to receive a heart transplant is a blessing and a miraculous gift. One of the doctors on the team reminded us that not many people make it on the list. "You and your family worked hard to get here and you deserve it."

 **Bridget Pinckney Dewees**

Transplant Education Pt 2: The organ transplant process is amazing! Believe it or not, when that organ finally comes in, they tell me it's like Christmas on the floor. Especially since the ICU staff has fallen completely in love with Jay. I must admit, we were scared of the thought of having a heart transplant, but through education, talking with several recipients and waiting while God conditioned us over several weeks, we are now anticipating this wonderful miracle. I heard Joel Osteen say that his Mom was healed from cancer the first time by the prayers of faith, but years later she experienced terrible hip pain. The doctors told her she needed a hip replacement. She prayed and prayed, stood on her faith, but God decided to heal her via medical treatment. It didn't mean she didn't believe, it didn't mean she didn't have faith and it definitely didn't mean God didn't do the healing. God has many ways of healing. The Bible says every good and perfect gift comes from Him. She went on to be pain free and is traveling the world. So, please don't offer pity or send, "I'm sorry!"

Get excited that Jay has this option on the table that could extend his life for decades and at a much higher quality than he has now. Get excited that God is doing His job and we are being led by Him. Get excited about the glory God will receive from us and those connected to us! What an honor to be chosen to give Him glory! This is why we are so calm. The peace of God has surpassed our own understanding and knowledge and is causing us not to perish. There is renewing going on while we wait, there is a shifting in our thinking and a healing of our mind! God is showing us that YOU CAN do all things through Him!

We believe we are close to our big miracle. The doctors are telling us how it works. The team has to fly or drive to lay eyes on the heart before they give final approval for Jay. Once approved, they totally prep Jay for surgery. All of this will happen within hours. I only have 1-2 hours to get to Jay. If I am not there, I won't see him before the surgery. (All I've got to say is I-26 better beware. lol). The actual surgery is about 4-6 hours. Within 24 hours they plan to have Jay sitting up in the recliner. Phase two, the recovery will be the most challenging part, but we have no doubt God will continue to amaze us and the doctors!

Human will is so amazing! I dare you to WILL yourself out of the situation you are in! Ask God to lead you to healing and believe you are coming out! Every single day is a faith walk, but with God I CAN!

# RECOVER BUT NEVER QUIT

## *Inspiration from James*

We wrote this book during our early recovery period at home. Yes, we were home and capturing all of these thoughts as a reminder of God's amazing grace. Recovery will be ongoing with major milestones over the next year. We are expecting the great and for God to continue to show us His healing power.

Our testimony gives us joy! As loved ones and dear friends come by to check on us, we find ourselves remembering even more details about the journey. I told my pastor about the phlebotomist who saw God at work right after leaving ICU. God has done a marvelous work and continued to show the medical field that He is in charge. I remember the doctors being concerned about my hemoglobin level, it was very low at one point. They did blood work the very next day and couldn't believe the results. They thought the phlebotomist mislabeled my blood for someone else. She explained, "Mr. Dewees was the only patient I had this morning. This is his blood." They said, "In order for this to be his blood, he would have had to have a blood transfusion and to please take it again. She came in to explain why she needed to stick me once more. I knew God was at work. The results the second time around showed even better results. I trust God!

I wrote one more journal to reflect on the meaning of recovery. I am truly in God's hands. I don't know about tomorrow, next week or next year, but I do know what God's Word says about our lives. We shall live to declare the works of the Lord. This was all for His glory! We have to recover, but we can't quit.

*Healing is a matter of time, but it is sometimes also a matter of opportunity.*

*Hippocrates*

## *Journal Entry #13*
## *Day 82: July 8ᵗʰ*

### *Recover But Don't Quit*

*Yes...recovery is a central part of healing, strength and endurance. It's where your body reforms to the strength that it once knew, in hopes that you can take it to the next level, if you choose to do so.*

*I had a pretty big blow through the transplant process, and although I knew I was touched by the hands of the Almighty God through the process, I could still feel the effects of the surgery. Therefore, it is essential for me to follow all of the rules and guidelines set before me by the doctors who assisted in this miracle in order for me to physically recover and be made totally whole.*

*We also realize that there was purpose through this transplant, and with the help of our God we're going to fulfill this purpose.*

*While in recovery mode your thinking shouldn't stop. This is the time to reflect, reminisce, and focus on the what's next. Seeking God for guidance and direction on the new you and what it would take for you to move forward, so that when you do recover physically you're also on the road to recovering every aspect of your life, fulfilling the destiny that God has called you to do. You recover, but you don't quit. You continue to press towards the mark for the prize of the high calling of God in Christ Jesus (Philippians*

3:14). *I'm looking forward to seeing the next opportunities in our lives!*

## Reflection from Bridget

Yes, room 8, the year 2018 and our 28th anniversary all represent a new beginning for the Dewees family! Jay was discharged just 10 days after the transplant. Prior to discharge, each patient participates in a bell ceremony to honor the organ donor and to give thanks for a second chance at life. Our dear friends ( Denise, Brenda and Chris), family and hospital staff were all there to hear and see Jay ring the bell. What a glorious day it was! We will be forever grateful for our new beginning.

 **Bridget Pinckney Dewees**

New Heart- New Normal

Post-Transplant: The humbling phase: When you lay your hands on the incision site and realize someone else's organ (via a loss of life) is helping you live and God's grace and mercy allowed it to be! How God strategically timed it all. How He kept Jay strong as possible with a very sick heart and said NOW is the Time! I think I'll live in this phase the rest of my life!

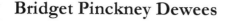 **Bridget Pinckney Dewees**

To whom much is given, much is required! Today, Jay went in for his first out-patient checkup. That heart is pumping strongly and doing exactly what it's supposed to do. Just amazing! I couldn't help but find my way to the waiting room to see if God needed me to share His love and our testimony. I ran across a family waiting while their Dad was having a heart transplant. I could see the nervous tension all over the young teen son. I told him we have a 15 year old and his dad just had a heart transplant, too. I gave him my phone to watch Jay's bell ceremony. I told him with a little bit of faith, this will be your Dad soon. Their faces lit up and he said, "I heard about him already—he waited 65 days in ICU!" Yes, this trial has purpose and I'm so humbled to be used by God to lift and encourage. Each of us has something that can help the next person. God designed His world to be that way. What a beautiful day! Keep praying for everyone dealing with tough challenges. Keep sharing your testimonies—they really help others overcome!

---

This book only captures a small part of the impact that this journey will have on our lives. I am so humbled to be used in this way. I will never take it for granted. The words of Dr. Ramu rings so loudly in my head every day. She reminded us that a loss of life granted this gift. So many would trade places and we are never to take it for granted. She told us we deserved the gift and was selected because of the work we put in to get it. Yes, this is the most humbling experience I have ever gone through. I tried to get back to normal, only to realize that there is no going back. God shifted us and we will never be the same.

*I thank God for hearing our specific prayers! For giving us peace, specifically Jay—for the right heart, and for a successful procedure and recovery! I see you God!*

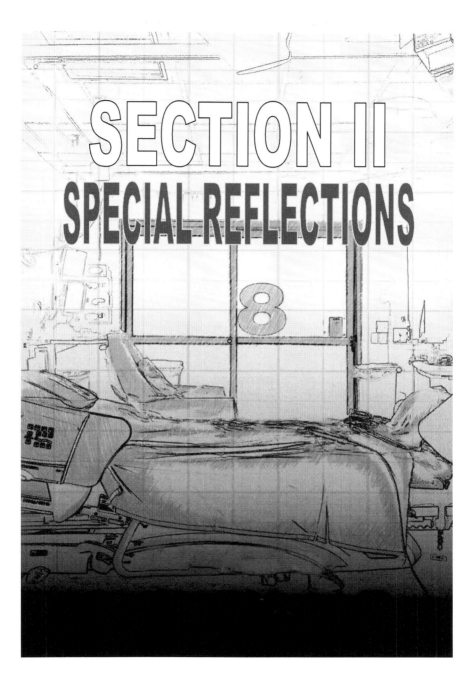

# REFLECTIONS AS A WIFE AND MOM

### Bridget Pinckney Dewees

Jay is such a special guy, he's a giver, lifter and role model to so many young men! You won't find him in messy issues or creating problems for others. People love being around him. I love watching him with Justin; they are best buds! His standards are high, but they are God's standards. From the day I met him singing Douglas Miller and Timothy Wright classics to this very day, his faith in God has been consistent! We've had challenges and several disappointments over these 28 years, but God has given us favor that exceeds any hurts! I love this guy, but you know that—he's the biggest part of my story!

God gave us this miracle on our 28th anniversary weekend. That wasn't a coincidence. He wants us to realize that we were called as a couple to give Him glory in the earth. We are living in a time where the institution of marriage has been discounted to just a piece of paper. God again, reminded me of the importance of the vows and how He honors couples who honor Him with their lives.

From the day I met Jay, I knew he was called to do something great in the Kingdom of God. Jay struggled with this call and didn't always have the confidence to walk in it. He doubted himself many times, but through this trial Jay showed me more of who God really is. I was there when they pulled the breathing tube out. Jay woke up praising God! Shortly after the removal of his breathing tube he said, "All the way from the beginning, I trusted God." I have never seen such strength and confidence in all the years we were together. His faith was so strong.

We would have prayer every night, even if by FaceTime. One night, he led the prayer and said, "Lord thank you for healing me, if you heal the heart I have, or decide to give me a new heart." Jay was in ICU, but ICU was not in him. I would often prepare a home-cooked meal and bring it to him. We did everything we could to make this journey as normal as possible.

God allowed me to see deeply into the soul of the man He

called to give Him glory. I posted a note about how opposite Jay and I are. Jay was in room 8, and outside of that room was a picture of an old timey "Praise House." After about a month, the nurses offered to let Jay move to a room with the best view on this floor and he said, "No thanks. I'm satisfied." I couldn't understand why, but I realized Jay coped with his situation by not worrying about what's outside or things he could not do. What a lesson for us all. Many of us are coping the wrong way. He already knew the beauty of what's to come, but he'd rather not let it taunt him every day for no reason right now. Focus on what you have control over! Jay was the epitome of waiting patiently!

### Bridget Pinckney Dewees

"Praise is What I do" Jay is handling his extended stay remarkably well! If anyone comes in his room with a pity party, including nurses, he quickly shifts the atmosphere! Remember, this the "praise house" as noted by the picture hanging outside his room (God is so strategic). The nurses take him on short walks outside to the atrium to get a breath of fresh air and sit in the sun now and then. He is not a fan of the 10 ways they serve chicken, but is making it work! Yesterday, we had a grilled seafood meal and it was ok—taste buds are weird. He keeps his mind clear and focused on the mission—that's how he put it yesterday. "This is a mission." Many have said to me, you are amazing for how you manage this all; but Jay is really the amazing one! His faith is strong and his trust in God is sure! Several of his childhood church buddies have stopped by to see him, he laughs and have fun and then checks them—he wants to know how is your walk with God. He encourages everyone to remember, everything can change in a minute without notice—always be ready my friends. Jay is someone special and God's favor rests on him. He is a real minister in his own right, even from a hospital room he is helping others! Keep those specific prayers going up!

I would get messages from Jay in the early hours of the morning. They were usually his journal or a message that God had given him throughout the night, but this post was special. After about a few weeks into the journey, Jay wanted to share his appreciation for all I was doing to see him through this. Of course, I had to share this on my Facebook Page.

**Bridget Pinckney Dewees**

Woke up to this special text from Jay: "I know that I don't say this enough, considering all that we've recently been through, but I want you to know that I truly, from the bottom of my heart, I appreciate you and all that you have done and are doing thus far. You're truly a gemstone given to me from God. I am wholeheartedly indebted to you and I thank God that he placed you in my life. What an honor to have you as my wife and partner. I am a very Blessed man! With genuine love, 💕 Jay"

## I.C.U. God

We spent June 23rd, 2018 in ICU listening to Jay's new heart. We were just kids when we said, "I do." One thing I can say is, we have honored our vows. I did not marry a perfect man—I married a man who first loved God with his whole heart and loved me, too. Over the years, that one attribute really was the glue. When a man/woman truly loves God, he/she loves their spouse and family with the love of God. As I watch Jay handle this heart transplant process, the most difficult challenge yet—and he has had some challenges, but I see God all over him. I see everything he has ever ministered, sang or played about come to life in this hospital room. He may have a moment here and there, but he is consistent in his faith and he lets the love of God shine through to the doctors, nurses and visitors. Folks come in nervous and leave there so much better and full of faith.

There is no doubt, God has a plan for all of this. Jay isn't the only one going through this healing process. There is some type of healing going on in everyone connected to Jay—including me. We are all going to be so much better and a lot stronger because of this journey. I celebrated our anniversary with a special tribute to Jay. I will never forget number 28 as long as I live.

**Bridget Pinckney Dewees**

When you say "I do"....Tribute to Jay

God is great and greatly to be praised—our 28th Anniversary is today! Last night we listened to Jay's new heart beating loudly and stronger than ever! We both looked so baffled, our eyes said, "How Lord, why us?" Many nights over the last 28 years, I've laid on your chest listening to your heartbeat, I knew the sound and I heard the decline these last few years, but I said, "I do." In sickness and health, for richer or poorer! I married a strong man, because my goal from the beginning was to make sure he loved God first—I knew he would love me. We are not perfect, we've had our times, but we said, "I do!" Jay has been committed to me for 28 years! He's been a consistent rock and my best friend. We grew up together, he let me be me!

Many are calling me amazing and strong for being by Jay's side, and I respond in my mind with, but I said, "I do!" Jay, these last 68 days, you showed me just how much you love God, you've strengthened my faith in ways you will never know. You fought for us, for Justin and for the Kingdom! I was there when you woke up from the heart transplant, and as soon as the breathing tube came out, you immediately began to praise God— I saw the Jay I married at his strongest! I promise, each time I hear this new heart beat, to be reminded of God's faithfulness to us!

Yes, I said, "I do" and with God, I will see you through this too! Happy Anniversary, I Love my Jay!

In ICU, God showed me that I had a great marriage. There

were times I wished he was more of this and I was more of that. So many times I did sweat the very small stuff. Over the years I took for granted the greatness of hanging in there and getting through life with a godly man. I encourage every married couple to look again and let go of the what ifs, the small stuff and embrace your great marriage.

### Bridget Pinckney Dewees

What if a great marriage is simply two people who committed to be there through the good and bad, two people having very different personalities, who are always on a journey of self-discovery, two people who sometimes bump heads, but love God with their whole hearts—so God constantly shows them how to love each other through disappointments, disagreements and very hard times.

What if a great marriage is making each other feel like no one else has ever made you feel, making each other so mad and then loving each other so hard it turns to GLAD.

What if a great marriage is living a very average life that takes a lot of work... what if a great marriage is two people simply never giving up on each other, and always looking at their God-given potential instead of their human flaws...

what if you are missing a great marriage, looking for fairy tale of happily ever afters...

**Thanking God for the valuable lessons learned as a wife, mother and caregiver.**

## JUSTIN WAS GOING THROUGH THIS, TOO

We have a fifteen year old son who was in his last weeks of 9th grade when James went in the hospital. Justin was very familiar with the hospital scene; he was only nine when this congestive heart failure journey started. He saw a strong Dad who always came home. He expected the same this time, but now we were dealing with the "teen years." I quickly realized that kids will handle life the best way they see fit without proper guidance, but this Mom was not going to let her son fail the last quarter of 9th grade. It was easy to say, give Justin a pass, this is tough and its easier on me to not worry about it, but Jay and I said we are ALL coming out victorious. I would spend days at the hospital or at work and nights at the kitchen table hovering over a very unfocused Justin. You see, Justin decided that he would just enjoy life his way and forfeit everything he had worked for. Many might have said, he gets a pass, but we decided that life doesn't give passes and Justin had one job; to finish his first year of high school successfully. I was very transparent and shared this very real post about re-focusing Justin.

 **Bridget Pinckney Dewees**

So, about my famous Facebook son Justin—we can't forget that he is going through this, too. Yes, we have expectations for him, but they are not higher than his capabilities. Immediately when Dad went in the hospital, Justin decided that he would just stop doing anything that wasn't NBA, including school work. I saw his A/B grades plummet to C/D/F! I grappled with how to balance what's necessary for him to get through 9th grade and how to make sure he's ok with what was happening to his family. Justin is a calm kid and handles hard things like an old man most times. He was only 9 when this CHF journey started. He's not afraid at all of the hospital scene—and he enjoys spending weekends with his Dad. I had to make sure Justin understood that when life gets tough, you get tougher! But like most teens, he can be an opportunist, and it was easier to shift to something he loves NBA. At least, it wasn't booze and girls. So Dad, Papa, Grandma, Uncle and Auntie jumped in on the "get it together" Justin talks—but it wasn't until I pulled the technology and cable plugs that he understood the importance of finishing strong! He had to make the connection that he still needs to do his part to keep things going. So, I was wife and or employee by day- and strong arm Mom by night! I sat at the kitchen table many nights after being in the hospital all day just to help him focus! I'm talking to plenty of Moms just like me—We do what it takes! Today, I pulled up his grades to see 4As, 2Bs and that C in math. Yes! Tough love won. Parents, children understand life more than we give them credit for! We kept our eyes and ears open to make sure we truly knew what's going on in his mind. We know what he is capable of and we couldn't let him down. Justin will be prepared to carry the torch. Y'all keep praying for us. We need it.

---

We spent several holidays in the hospital while on this journey. Mother's Day, Father's Day, Memorial Day, and our 28th Anniversary all occurred between April 18-July 2. My favorite holiday was Father's Day this year. I realized how great of a father Jay has been. I watched Justin try to step in his big shoes many of days. Many times, we think kids are not watching us, but they are. Boys become men by what they see, not what they hear. I saw this so clearly in Justin.

### Bridget Pinckney Dewees

Happy Father's Day to my Jay! Although you are away on the heart transplant journey—The love and lessons he poured into our son came alive these last two months! I can't tell you how many times Justin said "my Dad taught me that" from personal grooming to even the way he takes the time to turn his clothes inside out before washing them. The way he jumps out of bed 6:30 a.m. to roll the trash out, because I forgot, the way he questions me about strangers who speak to me, the way he asks me do we really need to buy that in Walmart. He heard me talking about something I wanted to do and he said—you have to make sure Dad is on board, Mom—as I rolled my eyes. I knew he was right! Oh and the way he won't let me go to sleep without praying together is all Dad! Justin knows exactly what his Dad would do or wouldn't do. Boys become good men because of what they see, not what they hear! Thank you for being a fantastic example! Yes, teens butt heads with Dad but during the challenges they become what they've seen! You've done a fantastic job with our gift! And for that I'm proud to say Happy Father's Day!

---

Justin has his own special testimony, he will realize that he was called to be a part of this great miracle and that God wants to use him for His glory too. I am really proud of Justin for giving up everything to assist Dad in recovery. He will never forget summer 2018! All transplant patients receive a special pillow that friends and family can sign. Justin signed Dad's pillow, "Thank you for being great." Justin our gift, may you always know how much Dad and Mom loves you!

---

 **Bridget Pinckney Dewees**

Post-Transplant Education:
What a wonderful feeling to be on the other side of a successful transplant! Just to hear Jay share his testimony on the phone with friends—is amazing! We are relaxing at

a local hotel close to the hospital, but our doctor approved us to go home. You have to be no more than 45 minutes away for 3 months and we just made the cut off! This process is so serious! You are on a nationwide waiting list so expectations are very high. Jay had to verify that he has primary and secondary caregivers, $5,000 on hand for immediate expenses, and that he is both emotionally and physically ready to handle this gift. They actually ask for a copy of your resources. All of this happens before you are approved. Post-transplant—now we are on a defined regimen that includes meds, diet, rehab, and weekly checkups with the cardiologist. The anti-rejection medications lowers the immune systems so the heart is tricked into becoming a normal part of the body. This also makes him vulnerable to catching colds and viruses more easily at this time. It will get better and he will get stronger with time. He is out and about with his mask, and is asked to avoid large crowds for a while. I bought so much anti-bacterial products this week, the cashier was looking at me side-eye. He is on driving restrictions for 8 weeks. While the heart is working great, his sternum takes 3 months to fully knit. Consequently, he is not supposed to lift more than 5-10 lbs. right now! So, the work begins and as we both agreed at the bell ceremony. We will never take this precious gift for granted. It has purpose! I will be taking a break from updates to enjoy the family for a few days. Be back soon! Love y'all and keep praying those specific prayers!

---

The work is in the recovery. We are writing this book while Jay is in recovery and healing mode. This is part two of the final exam. There are even more lessons that God wants me to learn about being a caregiver, a wife, and submitting my will for the good of the family. Jay's cardiologist, Dr. Vanbakel, told us, "In order to come out, you have to go through," and that is exactly what we are doing. We look forward to the other side of through!

# SECTION III
# THE PROMISES OF GOD

8

# GOD'S WORD FOR THE JOURNEY

A Word for the Journey - Scriptures we stood on while waiting on the promises of God.

| | |
|---|---|
| Acts 17:28 | For in him we live, and move, and have our being; as certain also of your own poets have said, For we are also his offspring. |
| 2 Corinthians 4:17-18 | For our light affliction, which is but for a moment, worketh for us a far more exceeding and eternal weight of glory; While we look not at the things which are seen, but at the things which are not seen: for the things which are seen are temporal; but the things which are not seen are eternal. |
| Hebrews 11:1 | Now faith is the substance of things |

|                  | hoped for, the evidence of things not seen. |
|---|---|
| Hebrews 12:1-3   | Wherefore seeing we also are compassed about with so great a cloud of witnesses, let us lay aside every weight, and the sin which doth so easily beset us, and let us run with patience the race that is set before us, Looking unto Jesus the author and finisher of our faith; who for the joy that was set before him endured the cross, despising the shame, and is set down at the right hand of the throne of God. For consider him that endured such contradiction of sinners against himself, lest ye be wearied and faint in your minds. |
| Hebrews 13:5     | Let your conversation be without covetousness; and be content with such things as ye have: for he hath said, I will never leave thee, nor forsake thee. |
| Isaiah 26:3      | Thou wilt keep him in perfect peace, whose mind is stayed on thee: because he trusteth in thee. |
| Jeremiah 29:11   | For I know the thoughts that I think toward you, saith the LORD, thoughts of peace, and not of evil, to give you an expected end. |
| 2 Kings 20:1-6   | In those days was Hezekiah sick unto death. And the prophet Isaiah the son of Amoz came to him, and said unto him, |

Thus saith the LORD, Set thine house in order; for thou shalt die, and not live. Then he turned his face to the wall, and prayed unto the LORD, saying, I beseech thee, O LORD, remember now how I have walked before thee in truth and with a perfect heart, and have done that which is good in thy sight. And Hezekiah wept sore. And it came to pass, afore Isaiah was gone out into the middle court, that the word of the LORD came to him, saying, Turn again, and tell Hezekiah the captain of my people, Thus saith the LORD, the God of David thy father, I have heard thy prayer, I have seen thy tears: behold, I will heal thee: on the third day thou shalt go up unto the house of the LORD. And I will add unto thy days fifteen years; and I will deliver thee and this city out of the hand of the king of Assyria; and I will defend this city for mine own sake, and for my servant David's sake.

Matthew 6:34 — Take therefore no thought for the morrow: for the morrow shall take thought for the things of itself. Sufficient unto the day is the evil thereof.

Philippians 1:6 — Being confident of this very thing, that he which hath begun a good work in you will perform it until the day of Jesus Christ:

Philippians 3:14 — I press toward the mark for the prize of the high calling of God in Christ Jesus.

| | |
|---|---|
| Philippians 4:8 | Finally, brethren, whatsoever things are true, whatsoever things are honest, whatsoever things are just, whatsoever things are pure, whatsoever things are lovely, whatsoever things are of good report; if there be any virtue, and if there be any praise, think on these things. |
| Proverbs 3:13-15 | Happy is the man that findeth wisdom, and the man that getteth understanding. For the merchandise of it is better than the merchandise of silver, and the gain thereof than fine gold. She is more precious than rubies: and all the things thou canst desire are not to be compared unto her. |
| Proverbs 4:23-24 | Keep thy heart with all diligence; for out of it are the issues of life. Put away from thee a froward mouth, and perverse lips put far from thee. |
| Psalms 34:15 | The eyes of the LORD are upon the righteous, and his ears are open unto their cry. |
| Psalms 34:22 | The LORD redeemeth the soul of his servants: and none of them that trust in him shall be desolate. |
| Psalms 23 | The LORD is my shepherd; I shall not want. He maketh me to lie down in green pastures: he leadeth me beside the still |

waters. He restoreth my soul: he leadeth me in the paths of righteousness for his name's sake. Yea, though I walk through the valley of the shadow of death, I will fear no evil: for thou art with me; thy rod and thy staff they comfort me. Thou preparest a table before me in the presence of mine enemies: thou anointest my head with oil; my cup runneth over. Surely goodness and mercy shall follow me all the days of my life: and I will dwell in the house of the LORD forever.

| | |
|---|---|
| Psalms 27:14 | Wait on the LORD: be of good courage, and he shall strengthen thine heart: wait, I say, on the LORD. |
| Psalms 22:3-5 | But thou art holy, O thou that inhabitest the praises of Israel. Our fathers trusted in thee: they trusted, and thou didst deliver them. They cried unto thee, and were delivered: they trusted in thee, and were not confounded. |
| Revelation 12:11 | And they overcame him by the blood of the Lamb, and by the word of their testimony; and they loved not their lives unto the death. |
| Romans 5:1 | Therefore being justified by faith, we have peace with God through our Lord Jesus Christ: |
| Romans 8:18 | For I reckon that the sufferings of this |

|  |  |
|---|---|
|  | present time are not worthy to be compared with the glory which shall be revealed in us. |
| Romans 8:28 | And we know that all things work together for good to them that love God, to them who are the called according to his purpose. |
| Romans 8:37 | Nay, in all these things we are more than conquerors through him that loved us |
| 2 Timothy 1:7 | For God hath not given us the spirit of fear; but of power, and of love, and of a sound mind. |

# SECTION IV
# SOCIAL MEDIA'S ROLE

# BRIDGET'S TESTIMONIALS AND ENCOURAGEMENT FROM OTHERS

Social media played a huge role in our transplant journey. We were able to receive from and give encouragement to thousands. So many of our friends validated that God was with us and that we were chosen to give Him glory, even over the internet.

I have been a Facebook fan for years, and I couldn't stop now. I know many who are not as transparent or open with sharing hard journeys, but God told me to always tell this story and give Him the glory and I would never have to worry about anything. For the last seven years, I have been doing just that. On every platform God gives me, I find a way to share it. I have given out books at business conferences, church conventions or even in the hair and nail salons. I get strength when I share the goodness of God. James decided to join the social media train, too. He quickly realized that the responses from friends and family gave him a sense of purpose. He was encouraged and strengthened by the brothers and sisters online.

---

**Bridget Pinckney Dewees**
Folks who talk badly about social media, are not using it the right way! Wow, the notes and prayers sent to us across this page are just amazing! Please forgive me if I don't respond right away, but I see you! Jay asked me to read your comments to him today and a huge smile came across his face! Thank you all for lifting us!

---

I would share all of the interactions and keep everyone updated on Jay's progress. I was very transparent. I let others see the real thoughts and struggles as well. I was lifted by this wonderful tool. There are many with ill intentions, but the Lord reminded me that no weapon formed against us will prosper. We are free to roam around the country when we are doing God's will for our lives.

**Bridget Pinckney Dewees**

Jay is making such an impact in this hospital! We met Nurse Heather in the lab on Day 1 when we first found out that he needed to stay in the hospital. She is new in the faith and told us that she can't stop praying for a heart for James Dewees. Today, she found us to confirm that it's time to get excited—she repeated many things from my post last night as confirmation! She said, "I came in here to lift James and y'all just encouraged me." That's been the story of this journey—helping lift others and God blesses us! I gave her a copy of our first testimony. God is up to something big! Pray for her family and that God continues to strengthen her faith.

## Actual posts from friends (unedited)
## April – June 2018

Jay wasn't a Facebook person, but look how he's using the tool now to bless so many.

---

On another note... I read your post and when I say you spoke to my spirit!! We always see people willing to share their "Highs" and accomplishments, but we never get to see the daily struggles, obstacles, and real life issues WE ALL HAVE! What you did in that one post took so much courage, strength, and most importantly vulnerability (all things that make you the beautiful woman you are). I know for me it made me (1) stop and pray for strength and healing for your husband and family, and (2) remind myself to keep things in perspective.

You guys are such role models for so many. Your love and commitment to each other has stood as a testimony for the Lord Jesus Christ. That love will not fail in this moment and most of all God will honor His word and the sacrifice from both of you as servants and ambassadors for the Lord Jesus Christ. A miracle is on the way. Keep the faith Bridget Pinckney Dewees and family. love yall dearly.

To God Be The Glory!!! But/Only God!!! Especially this being 7 years after Brother Jay Lazarus Experience in 2011 and now 2018!!! Completion it is 7 years later!!! About to walk with a New Beginning Miracle Heart!!! To God Be The Glory!!! Praising God with Tears of Total Joy Jesus!!!! My Forever Miracle Family!

Jay is a Very Special Man! Lifting each of you in Prayer. Especially you Bridget God has Grace you to be who you are and God's strength will see you through sis.

Continue to bless others with your testimony. Sis you and your family have the favor of God all over you. We just love you all and you truly inspire us as a newly married couple.

There are some that talk the talk; and others that walk the walk. My dear sister, keeping on walking and being a true reflection of God. Through the Dewees Family there is a blessing for us all !

Such a inspiration for all of us! You guys were chosen for this bc He knew you could handle it. Continued blessings to you, Jay and Justin.

I love you, Bridget! Jay is in my prayers. God is in control. Rest in the fact that God is sovereign. His ability to be omnipresent, omnipotent, and omniscient is such a big blessing for His children. Don't you worry; He will heal, and He will reward you and Jay for your unwavering faith. Keep pressing forward.

Praise God sis Bridgette thank you for sharing Jay's message, I let some of the ladies in my prayer warriors group know who are agreeing in prayer for his victory and this is what she wrote in response to his lovely message.... please tell Jay he is an encouragement to me today as I read his words tears came to me because it's confirmation of what we have learned this quarter in small group. God is simply amazing....he's still encouraging others through his faith and strength tell him ...God bless...

I'm literally in tears reading this post. Words from you and Jay are ministering to my peace.
I'm still praying. Your perspectives give hope to any situation any of us have to face.
You're an inspiration to and for all to see.
Prayers continue for you and your family.

Good morning and God bless you and your family continually. Instructions well- said, Dr. Dewees (Smile). You are one awesome Woman of God. Your faith walk is certainly one which mirrors the love and patience of Christ. You your husband, and son are blessed to be used of the Holy Spirit to carry and so boldly share such life- changing testimonies of God "Sustaining Healing Power. The God-kind of Faith speaks, decrees and declares VICTORY in spite of - I thank God the both your husband are carriers of such faith. I believe. There's a vast amount of people being encouraged and blessed by your level of faith in God and the testimonies you each share. Keep up the great work ; and know that your labor of love is not in vain. You're in my prayers consistently. Love you much.

---

Love it!!! Keep the encouraging words coming...some may never answer your post but it may meet a need in their life, home and family!! Praying continually and specifically for the Dewees family.

---

Ma'am you are encouraging us thru your trial! I pray you continue to gain strength from the prayers going up for yall.

---

You are special!! God bless you! I may not k now you but I do because of who you are and both of you all sharing grace....humility.... and love!

---

Soror Bridget, I look forward to seeing your texts. You have no idea how uplifting they are to me. May God continue to give you the strength to carry on.

---

Jay is not only there to get better but he's there to minister as well. Trust the process! It's not about Jay, it's about him giving the word to others. God bless you and the family.

---

God has a plan for each of us and I know sometimes we want to know every step we will take but we must always we remember that each of our steps are ordered by God. Everything he brings us to he also brings us though!!! It is all for his Glory!!!! So we say Yes!!!! And we say use me Lord for your Glory!!!!!God has it all in Control!!!! And we Bless his Name!!!!! Love you all much and always!!!! Tell Jay I'm going to make him a feast real soon!!!! Kisses for Justin, we miss you Guys!!!

---

The both of you are truly an inspiration for so many people! Thank you for being that light, not only encouraging yourself; but others as well.

---

You and Jay continue to be the most inspiring people I am honored to know. Prayers continue for all of you.

---

Maybe this journey has been extended because there are other lives you two are meant to touch. We both know about how God works with time.

The enemy fights you for where you are going, so raise your fight strategy!

---

The Lord is confirming it all! The perfect, healthiest heart that God has selected for Min. Jay Dewees is on the way in Jesus name!

---

Y'all should totally write another book with this journey. So encouraging.

---

God is a keeper and He has great things laid up in store for you!

---

God is Good. And Bridget you are a great person. Sweet spirit, and so pleasant. You have not changed. You have stood by your man to the end. God loves you and I praise you. He's a lucky man to have such a great woman. I will continue to pray for you both.

---

Omg I won't be able to sleep. I hope you have started a book Confirmation that We serve a living God. Bridget Pinckney Dewees you already know what I call you. Superwoman. Your strength is seen by all. Your Facebook lives kept us all connected. Jay is blessed to have you and God blessed you with Jay. Justin will reap the benefits I'm encouraged ❤friend.

God worked a miracle last night for my friend's husband. He received his new heart!! Praying for the family and every heartbeat. Also, praying for the family that gave him the gift of life. Praying for comfort for all. Bridget Pinckney Dewees, you and Jay are walking, talking, faith believing testimonies!!! God Bless!!

---

I can't stop smiling! The prayers of the righteous availeth much!!!!

---

God is able to do just what He said He would do!!!!!!!!! Hallelujah!!!!!! God be praised!!!!! He is HEALER!!!! I haven't been on Facebook and to open up and read about THIS!!!! GLORRRRRAAAAAYYYYYYYY!!!! So incredibly happy and thankful for your blessing!!!

---

You have no idea what an inspiration you and Jay have been to so many! Many of my family members and friends have prayed for you on a daily basis. Your constant faith has been uplifting and a witness to so many. I love you so much and am so incredibly happy that your sweet Jay will soon be back home with you and Justin and ready to chase away all those winged palmetto bugs for you!!!!!!!

---

You guys has been a blessing to all of us. Thanks for inviting us in to your world!! Stay strong!!

Well, talking from experience you have lifted my spirits many times at TTC. You can just walk in a room & spirits are lifted. This 'thing' that you, Jay & Justin (& the rest of your families) have been going through is absolutely huge. It's amazing to me that you both have been able to take time to keep us up to date. I know it probably has been a tool for you all too, to help yourselves to deal with all this. But know that it is helping many of us to deal with 'things' and keep going also. Bridget, you are an absolute 'dahhling'! I love you baby!

---

I am truly grateful for your transparent journey. You guys have blessed me in ways unexplainable. May God's Grace & Mercy continue to rest, rule & abide within the. Dewees household.

# ABOUT THE AUTHORS

### Bridget Dewees, PhD

Dr. Bridget Dewees is an award winning Quality Practitioner with more than 30 years of professional experience in Business, Finance, Organizational Development and Higher Education Administration. She is currently an assistant vice president for institutional effectiveness at Claflin University and an adjunct business professor. She is responsible for managing a comprehensive university-wide assessment program. She is also a quality practitioner providing several years of service to the national and state Baldrige programs.

Bridget is an entrepreneur and community service advocate. She is a public speaker and organizational development trainer. She has served on the Junior League of Charleston and Alpha Kappa Alpha Sorority Incorporated. Bridget released her first inspirational book in 2012, *A 21st Century Lazarus Experience* and a workbook for faith-based organizations in 2014, *Creating a Culture of Excellence in the Church*.

Bridget has a PhD in Management, from Walden University. She has a Master's degree in Business Administration from Webster University and a Bachelor of Science degree in Accounting from the University of South Carolina.

### James Dewees

James is a minister of music and the gospel of Jesus Christ! He is a motivator and example to many. Through his health challenges and healing, he shares with many that in spite of what comes our way, with God nothing is impossible! Over the years, he has ministered before thousands through the ministry of music! He has also had the privilege of singing the national anthem at two professional NBA games.

James is employed by the Boeing Company as a Lean Management System Coach/Practitioner. His responsibilities are focused on consulting, training, coaching and facilitating Boeing employees with the intent of improving processes within the employee's statement of work. Overall, James has more than 30 years of progressive experience in Manufacturing, Management and Employee Involvement.

James is also an entrepreneur with two published CDs; *Instrumental Praises*, a compilation of gospel greats done on the saxophone and *Coming Back Home*, a contemporary vocal CD of songs he penned. James has a Bachelor's of Arts in Business Management from Charleston Southern University and an Associates in Industrial Technology from Trident Technical College. He is currently assisting as a Minister at First Fruits Community Church in Summerville, SC.

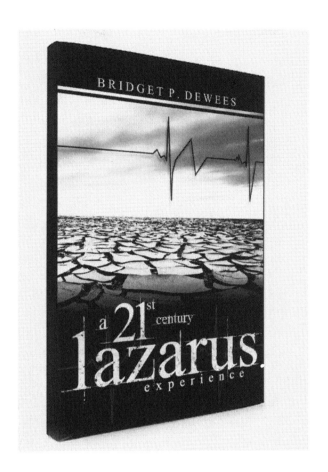

Join the journey—our first book, *A 21st Century Lazarus Experience* is available for purchase on www.amazon.com.

Made in the USA
Columbia, SC
23 November 2021